MW01141576

333.79   Tomljanovic, Tatiana.
TOM   Energy

SURREY SD# 36

4771016

Energy

Tatiana Tomljanovic

Weigl

CALGARY
www.weigl.com

Betty Huff Elementary
13055 Huntley Ave., Sry., BC V3V 1V1
LIBRARY

Published by Weigl Educational Publishers Limited
6325 10 Street S.E.
Calgary, Alberta T2H 2Z9

Copyright ©2008 WEIGL EDUCATIONAL PUBLISHERS LIMITED
www.weigl.com
All rights reserved. No part of this publication may be reproduced, stored in a retrieval system,
or transmitted in any form or by any means, electronic, mechanical, photocopying, recording,
or otherwise, without the prior written permission of Weigl Educational Publishers Limited.

Library of Congress Cataloging-in-Publication Data

Tomljanovic, Tatiana
    Energy / Tatiana Tomljanovic.

(Linking Canadian communities)
Includes index.
ISBN 978-1-55388-375-3 (bound)
ISBN 978-1-55388-376-0 (pbk.)

    1. Energy industries--Canada--Juvenile literature. 2. Energy
industries--Economic aspects--Canada--Juvenile literature. 3. Energy
industries--Canada--History--Juvenile literature. I. Title. II. Series.
HD9502.C32T64 2007   j333.790971   C2007-902262-6

Printed in the United States of America
1 2 3 4 5 6 7 8 9 11 10 09 08 07

Editor
Heather C. Hudak
Design
Warren Clark

All of the Internet URLs given in the book were valid at the time of publication. However, due to the
dynamic nature of the Internet, some addresses may have changed, or sites may have ceased to exist
since publication. While the author and publisher regret any inconvenience this may cause readers,
no responsibility for any such changes can be accepted by either the author or the publisher.

Photograph credits:
R.Garnett/Airscapes: page 3; **Syncrude:** pages 1, 10, 11 Top, 11 Bottom.
Every reasonable effort has been made to trace ownership and to obtain permission to reprint copyright
material. The publishers would be pleased to have any errors or omissions brought to their attention so
that they may be corrected in subsequent printings.

We acknowledge the financial support of the Government of Canada through the Book Publishing
Industry Development Program (BPIDP) for our publishing activities.

Contents

What is a Community?

A community is a place where people live, work, and play together. There are large and small communities.

Small communities are also called rural communities. These communities have fewer people and less traffic than large communities. There is plenty of open space.

Large communities are called towns or cities. These are urban communities. They have taller buildings and more cars, stores, and people than rural communities.

Canada has many types of communities. Some have forests for logging. Others have farms. There are also fishing, energy, **manufacturing**, and mining communities.

▶ Types of Canadian Communities

FARMING COMMUNITIES
- use the land to grow crops, such as wheat, barley, canola, fruits, and vegetables
- some raise livestock, such as cattle, sheep, and pigs

ENERGY COMMUNITIES
- found near energy sources, such as water, natural gas, oil, coal, and uranium
- have **natural resources**
- provide power for homes and businesses

FISHING COMMUNITIES
- found along Canada's 202,080 kilometres of coastline
- fishers catch fish, lobster, shrimp, and other sea life

Real Canadian Communities

Yellowknife
Northwest Territories
mining community

Fort McMurray
Alberta
energy community

Powell River
British Columbia
**forestry
community**

Shaunavon
Saskatchewan
**farming
community**

Oshawa
Ontario
**manufacturing
community**

Terence Bay
Nova Scotia
**fishing
community**

FORESTRY COMMUNITIES
- found near forests
- loggers cut down trees for building supplies and making paper

MANUFACTURING COMMUNITIES
- use natural resources to make a finished product
- finished products include cars and computers

MINING COMMUNITIES
- found in areas rich in **minerals**, such as zinc, nickel, and diamonds
- miners dig into the ground for minerals

Welcome to an Energy Community

Fort McMurray is an energy community. It is in northern Alberta. Fort McMurray began as a fur-trading post. It was built by the Hudson's Bay Company in 1870. Today, more than 60,000 people live here. Most of them work in oil and gas jobs. This is because Fort McMurray is found on the largest known crude, or unrefined, oil **deposit** in the world. It is called the Athabasca Oil Sands.

About 1.7 to 2.5 trillion barrels of crude oil are mixed in with the sand around Fort McMurray. Crude oil is a **fossil fuel**. It is a **non-renewable** source of energy. Crude oil is used to make gasoline. It helps cars and other vehicles to run. Crude oil is valuable. Some people who work in Fort McMurray take the crude oil out of the sand. Then they **refine** and sell it.

Oil sands are sent to extraction plants, where the oil is removed from the sand.

First-hand Account

Fort McMurray
Alberta
Pacific Ocean

N
0   200   400 kilometres
0   200   400 miles

My name is Carson. I live in Fort McMurray. We moved here from Newfoundland last year. My dad works in the oil patch. When we first arrived, my dad took us to the Oil Sands Discovery Centre. We watched a movie. It showed how oil is taken from the sand.

Last week I saw the biggest truck I have ever seen. It was three stories high. My dad says they cost $5 million to buy. It gets loaded up with oil sands. Then, it takes the load to a processing plant to make oil from the sand. Most of my friends have moved here from other parts of Canada, too. Some are from Newfoundland like me.

Think About It
Compare Fort McMurray to your community.
- **How is it the same?**
- **How is it different?**

The Energy Industry

Energy companies drill for oil and dig for coal. They are part of the energy industry. The energy industry also has factories and businesses that process natural resources. They turn them into forms of fuel or energy. The energy industry is important to many communities.

Energy is used to heat homes and businesses. It is used to power streetlights, cars, computers, and telephones. There are other energy sources, too. Wind power uses turbines to make energy. Like windmills, the turbine blade turns in the wind. It makes an electrical **current**. Wind and **solar** power are renewable energy sources. This means they can be used over and over again.

A wind farm is a group of 10 or more turbines in one place.

Timeline

500,000 BC
Humans begin to build fires.

1100 BC
Humans begin using coal as a fuel.

AD 1500
Leonardo da Vinci invents an oil lamp that has a glass chimney.

Solar power uses the Sun's rays to make energy. Solar panels trap the Sun's rays. The rays can be used to make heat and power.

The energy industry is important to Canadians. People work on rigs drilling for oil. They work in factories. Here, they turn crude oil into gasoline and **petroleum** products.

Hydropower is electricity made by the steam from heated water. In Manitoba, hydro lines transport electric power.

1881
Thomas Edison opens the first electricity-making plant in London, England.

1967
The Great Canadian Oil Sands plant becomes the world's first oil sands operation.

2002
Canada adopts the Kyoto Protocol. This is an agreement to reduce **greenhouse gases**.

Betty Huff Elementary
13055 Huntley Ave., Sry., BC V3V 1V1
LIBRARY

Crude Oil and Gasoline

The crude oil that is found in Canada has many uses. It provides fuel for cars and jet planes. It heats homes and powers factories. It even provides the raw materials for gasoline and plastics.

It is difficult to remove crude oil from the ground. Often, a hole is drilled into the ground. Sometimes, crude oil is mixed with sandy earth. To take the crude oil from the sand, large dump trucks carry loads of the sand and crude oil to refineries. A refinery is a type of factory. At the refinery, the oily sand is heated. This separates the sand from the crude oil. The oil is then made into a usable energy source, such as gasoline.

The CAT 797 is one of the biggest trucks in the world.

Gasoline Making Process

Plant and animal life die.

Their remains are buried in the ground for millions of years.

Layers of earth, heat, and pressure change the remains into crude oil.

People drill and dig into the ground. They remove the crude oil.

If the oil is mixed with sand, it is shipped by truck to a refinery. The oily sand is heated until it separates.

The crude oil travels through a **pipeline** to a refinery.

The refinery processes the crude oil into a usable energy source. Crude oil is processed into petroleum products.

Crude oil is processed into gasoline.

The gasoline is sold to companies. They sell it to car and truck drivers, pilots, and ship captains.

Canada's Energy Map

There are different sources of energy across Canada. Most of the energy comes from fossil fuels. Fossil fuels include crude oil, natural gas, oil sands, and coal. Canada also has uranium. It is a **radioactive** metal that is used to make **nuclear power**. Uranium comes from the Athabasca Basin in northern Saskatchewan. This map shows where uranium is found in Canada. It also shows other types of energy sources.

Legend

■ Current producing oil and gas basins

■ Current producing coal fields

■ Current producing uranium resources

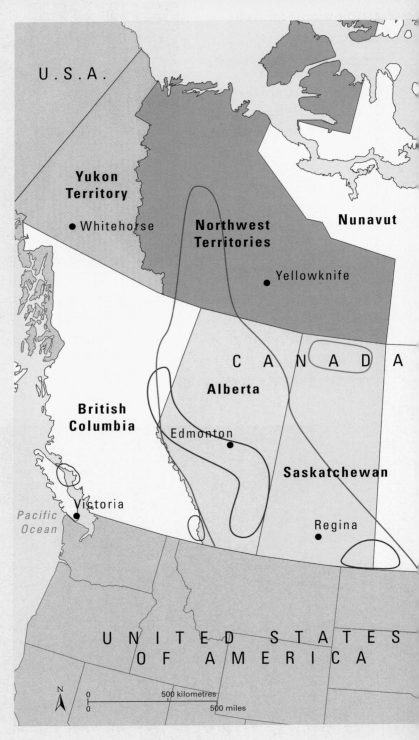

U.S.A.

Yukon Territory

● Whitehorse

Northwest Territories

Nunavut

● Yellowknife

C A N A D A

Alberta

British Columbia

● Edmonton

Saskatchewan

Victoria

Pacific Ocean

Regina ●

U N I T E D   S T A T E S
O F   A M E R I C A

N

0   500 kilometres
0   500 miles

Iqaluit

Labrador Sea

Hudson Bay

Newfoundland
and Labrador

Manitoba

St.
John's

Prince Edward
Island

Ontario

Quebec

Charlottetown

Winnipeg

New
Brunswick

Nova
Scotia

Quebec
City

Fredericton

Halifax

Ottawa ★

Toronto

Atlantic Ocean

Careers

Canada's energy industry makes many jobs for Canadians. Some of these jobs are petroleum engineer, oil well driller, and **utilities** manager.

The energy industry provides jobs for people who do not work directly in energy. Other businesses help store, ship, and sell energy sources. Oil and gas refineries help process raw materials. Raw materials are products that have not yet been made into something else. Drilling and digging need special machinery. Trucks, trains, and ships are needed to **transport** Canada's gasoline, coal, and uranium. All of these needs are supplied by businesses that have been set up to help the energy industry.

Petroleum engineers find better ways of improving drilling and digging for oil and gas. They study oil and where it is found. Then, they invent new ways to remove the oil from the ground quickly.

Oil well workers can make more than $100,000 a year.

Oil well drillers control the equipment that drills an oil well. These drills are called rigs. The drillers work outside. They set up, take down, and transport rigs between sites. They also care for the rigs. Drillers are the people who remove the oil from the ground. Drilling is difficult and sometimes dangerous work.

Utilities managers make sure that utilities are ready for people to use. People need utilities to heat and power their homes and businesses. Utilities managers decide how much to charge for utilities.

More than 300,000 Canadians work in the energy industry.

Oil and gas refineries operate 24 hours a day, seven days a week.

Think About It
What other jobs might there be in the energy industry?

Links Between Communities

Everyone is part of a community. It may be a village, a town, or a city. Communities are linked to one another. Each Canadian community uses goods that link it to other communities. Goods are things people grow, make, or gather to use or sell.

A forestry community makes lumber for construction. The wood may be shipped to another community to build houses or furniture.

Energy communities produce natural gas, oil, and other types of energy, such as wind, solar, and hydro. Other communities use this energy to power their homes and vehicles.

Dairy products and meats come from farming communities that raise cattle and other animals. People in all communities drink milk products and eat meat from these communities. Many farming communities grow crops such as wheat. Wheat is used to make bread and pastries.

These goods may be fish, grains, cars, and paper products. Communities depend on one another for goods and services. A service is useful work that is done to meet the needs of others. People are linked when they use the goods and services provided by others.

Manufacturing communities make products such as cars and trucks. They also make airplanes, ships, and trains that are used to transport, or move, people and goods from one place to another. Transportation services help communities build links.

Fishing communities send fish to stores to be bought by people in other places. In Canada, most fish is caught off the Pacific or Atlantic coast. People living on farms or in cities across the country buy the fish at stores.

Diamonds, gold, and potash can be mined. These items are sent from mining communities to other parts of the country. A diamond might be set in a ring for a person in another community.

Think About It
In your community, what goods and services help meet your family's needs and wants?

The Environment

O il, natural gas, coal, and uranium come from the ground. When they are taken out of the ground, the environment is often damaged. The animals that live there lose their homes. Plants that grow there are harmed.

The energy industry tries to find ways to remove natural resources without harming the environment. Still, when oil or coal is taken from the ground, the environment is changed. In the Athabasca oil sands, trees and **muskeg** are cleared away to reach the oil sands. When a company finishes mining, it fills the pit with leftover sand. The sand layer is covered with rock, sand, and clay. Then, grasses, shrubs, and trees are planted.

Oil refineries make large amounts of pollution.

Think About It
What would happen to your community if there were no more fossil fuels to provide electricity and gasoline?

The processing and use of fossil fuels causes air pollution. Pollution happens when chemicals get into the air. When people drive their cars or heat their homes, they burn fossil fuels. Burning fossil fuels produces greenhouse gases. These are a type of air pollution.

Fossil fuels, such as oil, gas, and coal, are non-renewable. Once they are used, they are gone forever. Canada uses many non-renewable resources. They make up 96 percent of Canada's energy. The energy industry is working to find better ways of drilling, digging, and processing. Over time, the non-renewable energy resources will run out.

Eco-friendly Renewable Resources

Canada has renewable resources that can make energy. Renewable resources are replaced by nature. Falling water, solar power, and wind power are renewable resources. Canada is the world's largest producer of hydropower. Hydropower is clean. It does not produce air pollution.

Brain Teasers

Test your knowledge by trying to answer these brain teasers.

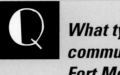

Q *What type of community is Fort McMurray?*

A Fort McMurray is an energy community.

Q *Name three types of communities in Canada.*

A Canada has forestry communities, farming communities, fishing communities, energy communities, mining communities, and manufacturing communities.

Q *What two things link communities?*

A Goods and services link communities.

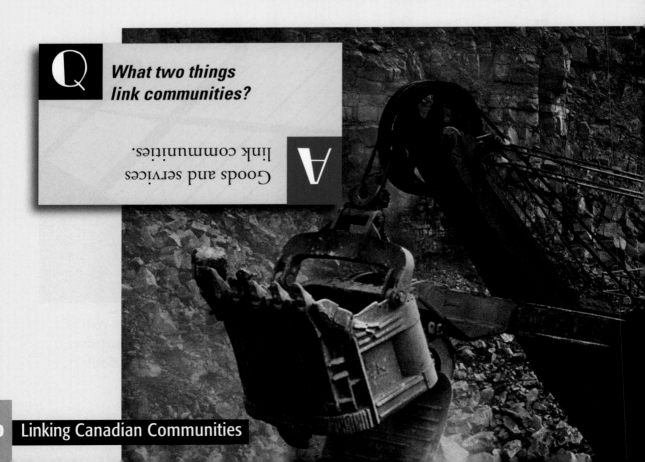

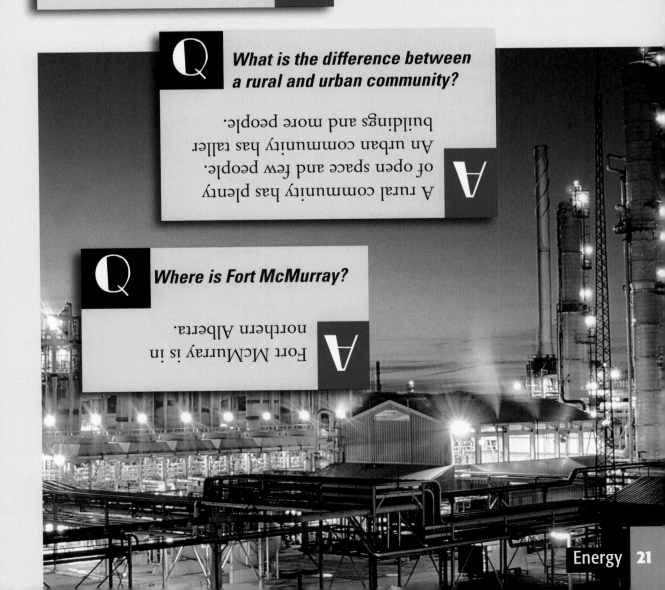

Q *What can crude oil be used to make?*

A Crude oil can be used to make gasoline and other petroleum products.

Q *What is the difference between a rural and urban community?*

A A rural community has plenty of open space and few people. An urban community has taller buildings and more people.

Q *Where is Fort McMurray?*

A Fort McMurray is in northern Alberta.

Solar-powered Cookout

Materials

- one tube-shaped potato chip can
- one hot dog wiener
- scissors
- one wooden skewer
- one 10 x 20 centimetre sheet of transparency film tape

Procedure

1. Cut an opening in the side of the can. To do this, make a 18-centimetre long slit in the centre of the long side of the tube and a 8-centimetre slit on each side of the long slit.
2. Cover the opening of the inside of the can with the film. Tape the film in place.
3. Make a small hole in the metal bottom of the tube. Make another in the plastic lid. Then, remove the lid.
4. Put the hot dog on the skewer, and place it inside the tube. Be sure to fit the skewer inside the hole in the bottom. Then, put on the lid.
5. Place the cooker in the sunlight. Make sure the flaps of the can are facing direct sunlight.
6. Time how long it takes your hot dog to cook.

Further Research

Many books and websites provide information on energy communities. To learn more about energy communities, borrow books from the library, or surf the Internet.

Books

Most libraries have computers that connect to a database for researching information. If you input a key word, you will be provided with a list of books in the library that contain information on that topic. Non-fiction books are arranged numerically, using their call number. Fiction books are organized alphabetically by the author's last name.

Websites

The World Wide Web is also a good source of information. Reliable websites usually include government sites, educational sites, and online encyclopedias.

Use an online community to find out more information about energy at **www.energyquest.ca.gov**.

To learn about energy facts and how energy works, check out **www.aecl.ca/kidszone/atomicenergy/index.asp**.

Information about Fort McMurray is available at **www.fortmcmurraytourism.com**.

Words to Know

current: the flow of electricity

deposit: a natural layer of sand, rock, coal, or other material

fossil fuel: an energy source formed from the remains of plants and animals that lived long ago

greenhouse gases: the air pollution created by the burning of fossil fuels

manufacturing: making a large amount of an item using machines

minerals: inorganic substances that are obtained through mining

muskeg: moss-covered swamp or bog

natural resources: materials found in nature, such as water, soil, and forests, that can be used by people

non-renewable: unable to be replaced in nature once they are used

nuclear power: power produced by splitting uranium atoms into parts

petroleum: thick oil found below Earth's surface that is made into gasoline, heating oil, and other products

pipeline: a system of hollow tubes hundreds of kilometres long used to transport oil

radioactive: to give off energy caused by the splitting of atoms

refine: to process crude oil to make it pure

solar: coming from the Sun's rays

transport: to move from one place to another

utilities: companies that supply gas, water, and electricity to the public

Index